FOR REUBEN AND GILES
- H.S

TO MY PARENTS, NEUZA, AND DONATO
- R.D

First edition published in 2023 by Flying Eye Books,
an imprint of Nobrow Ltd. 27 Westgate Street, London, E8 3RL.

Text © Helen Scales
Illustrations © Rômolo D'Hipólito
With special thanks to Jen Jones and The Galápagos Conservation Trust

Edited by Sara Forster
Designed by Sarah Crookes

1 2 3 4 5 6 7 8 9 10

Published in the US by Nobrow (US) Inc.
Printed in Poland on FSC® certified paper.

ISBN: 978-1-838748-59-3
www.flyingeyebooks.com

HELEN SCALES • RÔMOLO D'HIPÓLITO

SCIENTISTS IN THE WILD
GALÁPAGOS

FLYING EYE BOOKS

CONTENTS

WELCOME TO THE GALÁPAGOS

In the middle of the Pacific Ocean, out in the deep blue sea, lie a cluster of islands unlike any other. This is the Galápagos archipelago.

Most of the islands are shaped like cones. They are made from layer upon layer of molten lava that poured out of the volcanoes and cooled into black, jagged rocks.

The Galápagos Facts

- There are 13 main islands and more than 120 small islets, and they are very, very remote. The nearest mainland is Ecuador, 620 miles away to the east.

- All the islands were made by volcanoes. The oldest ones erupted around 5 million years ago. The youngest ones still occasionally erupt.

- The equator goes right through the islands. This should mean they are always tropical and hot, but there's more going on here. The Galápagos lies at a great meeting point in the ocean where warm currents come from the north and cold currents sweep in from the south and west. Like giant rivers, these currents mix and create an unusual climate where a unique mix of species has come together.

- The Galápagos is an incredible hotspot of biodiversity, home to thousands of species on land and in the sea. It's a gathering of wildlife like nowhere else on Earth.

The best way to explore these islands is by sailboat, especially for an adventurous team of scientists . . .

Human History of the Galápagos

The islands were officially discovered in 1535 by the Bishop of Panama. The story goes that he was sailing to Peru when he was swept off course by a strong ocean current that carried him to the islands. Ecuador claimed the islands in 1832.

The Galápagos became a national park in 1959, when only around 1,000 people lived here, most of them fishers. Now around 30,000 people live in the Galápagos and each year more than 250,000 tourists come to visit.

EXPEDITION GALÁPAGOS

Seven scientists from around the world have joined to study the wildlife of the Galápagos on board the research ship *Sula*. Each member of the team brings their own expertise to the expedition.

Saludos. I'm Catalina Maria Rosero. Call me Cata. I'm here mainly for the rocks!

Kon'nichiwa. My name is Ren Kobayashi. This is my first time visiting the Galápagos.

Hola. I'm Oscar Luna. I come to the Galápagos every year to listen to whales.

Cata is the team's geologist, a scientist who studies rocks, sediment,s and other physical structures that make up the earth. She is also a bio-geochemist, which means she studies the chemicals that are vital to life on earth.

Ren is an invertebrate biologist, a biologist who specializes in animals with no backbone, including corals, crabs, and sponges. She's also an expert on species that live deep underwater—a deep-sea biologist.

Oscar specializes in marine mammals like whales and sea lions. He's a marine mammologist. On this expedition he'll be working as an acoustic ecologist, studying the sounds of wild animals. Oscar is also a free diver, someone who swims deep underwater while holding their breath.

Davide is an ornithologist, a biologist who specializes in birds. He's also an evolutionary biologist, a scientist who studies how species evolve.

Tomas specializes in reptiles, like tortoises, turtles, snakes, lizards, and iguanas. He's a herpetologist. As a conservation biologist it is also his mission to help protect biodiversity and prevent species from going extinct.

Estefania is an oceanographer. She studies different physical aspects of the ocean, like currents and waves. As the team's deep-sea pilot, it's her job to drive the deep-diving submersible.

Leonora is an ichthyologist, a type of marine biologist who specializes in fish. She is also the team's underwater photographer so she'll be documenting underwater life on camera.

WELCOME ABOARD THE *SULA*

This is the research vessel *Sula*, where the crew will live, sleep, eat, and work for the next few weeks. Their mission is to sail from island to island to study and survey the incredible wildlife of the Galápagos, on land and in the sea.

1. Laboratory and specimen collection
2. Observation deck
3. Crow's nest (tiny platform up the main mast)
4. Library
5. Galley (kitchen)
6. Cabins
7. Captain's quarters

Sula is the scientific name for one of the Galápagos' colorful birds, the blue-footed booby.

8. Bridge (platform where the captain commands the ship)
9. Deep-diving submersible
10. Equipment room
11. Inflatable boat
12. Propeller
13. Engine room
14. Head (bathroom)

DIVING EQUIPMENT

To conduct their studies of the marine life around the Galápagos, the science crew use diving equipment to work at different depths underwater.

Snorkel

Diving mask

Regulator and spare regulator

Wetsuit

Dive computer

Buoyancy jacket

Weight belt

Air tank

Waterproof flashlight

Underwater cameras

Waterproof clipboard and pencils

Fins

Snorkeling equipment

Depth: Surface to 15 feet

Grabbing a mask, snorkel, and pair of fins is the simplest way to survey wildlife near the sea's surface. It's very useful because snorkelers can stay in for as long as they want. There's no time limit.

Scuba equipment

Depth: 15 feet to 100 feet

Scuba divers go deeper and study animals that can only be found at certain depths, such as sharks and red-lipped batfish. Depending on exactly how deep they go, scuba divers can stay underwater for around one hour at a time. They have to keep an eye on a dive computer, like a big wristwatch, which tells them how deep they are and how much time they have left from their air supply.

Deep-diving Submersible, *Kiwa*

Depth: Down to 19,700 feet (3.7 miles)

To go even farther down and study deep-sea species and ecosystems, scientists need to dive inside a submersible. These tightly sealed metal chambers have windows for seeing through and robotic arms controlled from inside that pick things up and conduct science experiments. The scientists can stay deep underwater for many hours, but of course they can't go outside!

Crane to winch it in and out of the sea

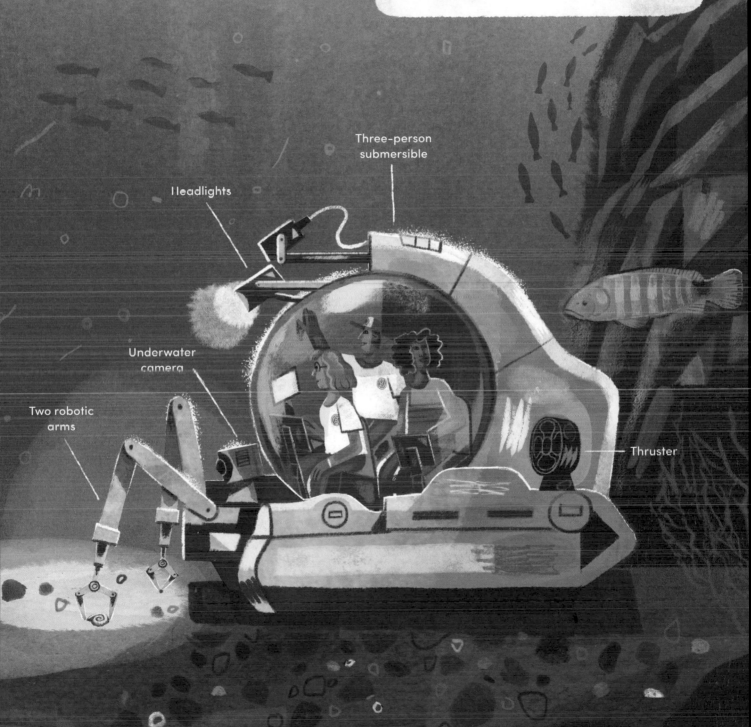

Three-person submersible

Headlights

Underwater camera

Two robotic arms

Thruster

GUIDE TO GALÁPAGOS LIFE

The Galápagos is home to its own special mix of wildlife, which is what makes this such an important and exciting place to study. Leo tells the *Sula* team about the species they'll encounter, including many that are endemic to the Galápagos—this is the only place in the world they live. These include: 30 percent of the plants in the Galápagos, 80 percent of the land birds, 97 percent of the reptiles, and 20 percent of the marine life.

Sadly, many species in the Galápagos are on the brink of going extinct. This is partly because many endemic species only live in a small population in a small area of habitat, which puts them at great risk of threats such as climate change, habitat loss, and introduced species.

Native species naturally live in a particular place.

80% of land birds in the Galápagos are endemic

30% of the plants in the Galápagos are endemic

Introduced species are plants and animals that people have brought in, either on purpose or by accident. There are more than 1,500 introduced species in the Galápagos. Many are harmless but a few, such as rats, cats, dogs, and goats, are a danger to native and endemic species.

97% of the reptiles in the Galápagos are endemic

Endemic species live in only one place.

Extinction Categories:

Scientists assess species and work out how close they are to extinction, based on how many are alive, how fast the population is shrinking, and the health of their habitat.

LC Least Concern
Unlikely to go extinct any time soon

NT Near Threatened
Close to being at high risk of extinction in the future

V Vulnerable
High risk of extinction

EN Endangered
Very high risk of extinction

CE Critically Endangered
Extremely high risk of extinction

EW Extinct in the Wild
Only alive in captivity

EX Extinct
No living members left

20% of marine life in the Galápagos is endemic

17

COUNTING PENGUINS

On the *Sula's* first stop, Fernandina Island, the team study the most famous swimming birds in the Galápagos—the penguins. The scientists' main task is to count all the penguins here. It's especially important to know how many young ones there are. If there are lots, it's a good sign the penguin population is healthy.

Young Paddlers

Good news! Almost half the penguins the *Sula* team spot at Fernandina are juveniles. This means the adults are breeding well.

Penguins swim slowly at the surface with their heads sticking out, making them easy to spot.

Juveniles look different to the adults. They don't yet have a white line on their cheeks or a dark band on their chests leading to their feet.

Speedy Divers

Penguins dive underwater to hunt for small fish, like sardines and anchovies. They can swim more than 20 miles per hour. The scuba divers' task is to photograph the penguins underwater as they whiz by.

Galápagos penguins
Pingüino de Galápagos

Size: 20–22 in.
Lifespan: 20 years
EN Endangered

Penguin ID

The pattern on a penguin's belly is like a fingerprint. Each penguin looks different. The *Sula* scientists have a digital catalog of photos showing all the penguins spotted by other scientists around Fernandina. By matching their photos to the catalog, they can figure out if the same penguins are here year after year. This also helps them work out how long the penguins here live.

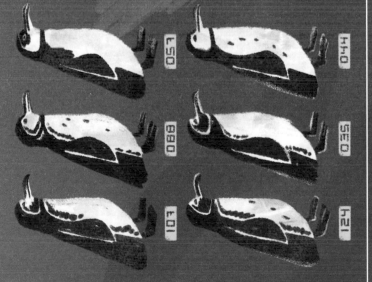

057 040
088 052
101 124

TAGGING A TIGER

Off Isabela Island, the *Sula* team search for one of the ocean's biggest hunters. Their mission is to fix a satellite tag on a tiger shark and track where it goes.

How to Track a Tiger Shark

To attract the sharks to the boat, the team throws buckets of rotting fish heads and guts into the sea. This mixture is known as *chum* and the sharks are attracted to the smell of it. When a tiger shark comes near, the scientists carefully catch it on a fishing line. Once the shark is next to the boat the scientist turns the shark upside down so it falls into a sleepy trance called *tonic immobility.* The shark is then measured from snout to tail and a satellite tag is fixed to its dorsal fin before the team releases it again.

Satellite Tag

This small gadget is like the GPS tracker in a cellphone. Fixed to the tiger shark, the tag records its location every 12 hours and pings the data to satellites in space, which then send them to Estefania's computer on the *Sula.* Joining the dots together, she draws maps of where the shark has been swimming.

Tiger shark
Tiburón tigre

Size: 18 ft. +
Lifespan: Unknown
NT Near Threatened

Sharks that Stick Around

Tiger sharks live in tropical and subtropical waters all around the world. In some places, they are migratory and go on long journeys for thousands of miles. But the *Sula*'s tagged shark doesn't swim very far at all. Along with other tiger sharks in the Galápagos, this one stays close to the islands where there's plenty of prey to hunt. Here in the Galápagos there are lots of green turtles. The Galápagos Marine Reserve is doing a good job of protecting the turtles and the tiger sharks from being caught in fisheries.

– Isabela Island –

Largest island in the Galápagos
Area: 1,803 mi²
Highest point: 1,061 ft.
Human population: 1,800

GIANT SWIMMING HEADS

At the northern tip of Isabela Island, diving off a rocky point called Punta Vincente Rosa, the *Sula* team have a surprising encounter. They are searching for bullhead sharks when they come across a huge shoal of sunfish.

Normally sunfish are loners and don't swim in shoals. But these ones are all visiting a cleaning station. Red and yellow hogfish are nibbling off bits of dead skin and parasites from them.

Sunfish
Pez luna

Size: Up to 11 ft.
Lifespan: Unknown
Ⓥ Vulnerable

Sunfish are the biggest bony fish in the world (although sharks can be bigger, they have skeletons made of soft cartilage not bone). Sunfish are voracious jellyfish eaters.

SMART HUNTERS

The *Sula* scientists stop at a cove on Isabela Island to study some very unusual behavior. A few years ago, local fishers noticed the Galápagos sea lions were hunting not for their usual prey, sardines, but were chasing yellowfin tuna. These are some of the fastest fish in the ocean. To catch them, the sea lions learned to team up. Oscar films the hunt underwater to learn more about what the sea lions are doing.

How to Catch a Tuna

Step 1: Between three and six sea lions patrol the narrow entrance to a cove.

Step 2: When a school of tuna swim by, the sea lions zigzag and porpoise, chasing the fish into the cove.

Sea lion
Lobo marino

Size: 6.5 ft. (female) 8 ft. (male)
Lifespan: 15–20 years
E Endangered

St 4: The sea lions drive the school even closer to shore, whipping the fish into a frenzy. The biggest sea lions eat first. Younger ones get the scraps and tails. Sharks, frigate birds, pelicans, and hawks all join in with the feast.

Step 3: Other sea lions block the cove's entrance, so the tuna can't escape. It's a trap!

Nobody is quite sure why they do this, but the sea lions of the Galápagos may have learned to hunt for tuna because sardines (their usual prey) are becoming harder to find as the sea gets warmer.

FLOATING TRASH

Out at sea, the *Sula* team spot two fishers hauling something out of the water into their boat. It's a tangle of floating wood and plastic. They motor closer to find out more.

Fish Aggregating Devices, or FADs, are an unsustainable way of fishing. Small fish swim in and shelter around FADs. Large fish, like tuna, swordfish, and sharks, show up to eat the small fish. Then, fishing boats with huge nets come and scoop them all up, as well as any turtles, dolphins, and sea lions that are there too. FADs aren't allowed inside the Galápagos Marine Reserve but sadly, big boats just outside the protected area use hundreds of them and they often drift in.

Small-scale fishing is allowed in some parts of the marine reserve, but only more sustainable methods for catching fish and lobsters. Instead of putting FADs (which the locals call *plantados*) in the sea, fishers collect them and recycle the plastic to make chicken coops and hammocks.

When the Galápagos Marine Reserve was set up in 1998 it was the second biggest in the world. Now it's the 33rd.

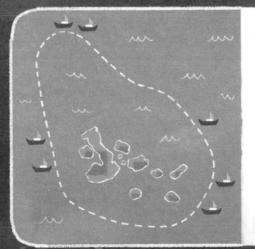

The waters around the Galápagos are well protected and full of marine life, but migratory animals aren't safe when they set off on their long journeys. Industrial fishing fleets wait just outside the reserve and sometimes catch the animals as they leave.

RARE AND PINK

Lots of different types of iguanas live in the Galápagos. One rare species is the pink land iguana. There's only about 200 of them left. All of them live on the slopes of Wolf Volcano on Isabela Island. The *Sula*'s science team set off on foot to count the rare iguanas and see how they are getting on.

Caught on Camera

Tomas sets up camera traps near the volcano's summit to investigate what's happening to the rare iguanas. He thinks it's likely that introduced rats and feral cats might eat their eggs and hunt for new hatchlings.

The iguanas are pink because their skin lacks color and their blood is visible underneath.

When Wolf Volcano erupted in 2015, the lava flowed to the east and southeast, avoiding the population of pink iguanas to the north and west. In 2022, Wolf erupted again and luckily missed the iguanas.

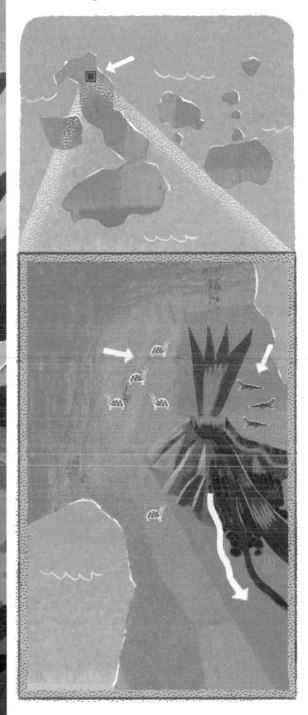

Very little is known about this species. Pink iguanas feed on prickly pear leaves and fruit.

Pink land iguana
Iguana rosada

Size: 4 ft.
Lifespan: Unknown
CE Critically Endangered

– Wolf Volcano –
Formed less than 500,000 years ago.
Height: 5,600 ft.

TINY, VITAL WONDERS

Sailing south and weaving through the islands, the *Sula* team study tiny creatures in the open sea. These microscopic life forms, called *plankton*, hold some of the biggest, most important secrets to the amazing life around Galápagos.

A deep, cold ocean current sweeps toward the Galápagos from the west. It's called the Equatorial Undercurrent and when it slams into the islands it sweeps upward to the surface, bringing lots of nutrients that feed great blooms of phytoplankton. The effect is like pouring fertilizer onto crops on land to help them grow. A rich soup of plankton feeds the bounty of marine life around the islands.

Phytoplankton get eaten by zooplankton.

Zooplankton get eaten by sardines.

Sardines get eaten by sea lions and penguins.

Infinitesimal Investigations

The *Sula* team lower down fine nets to catch two types of plankton—phytoplankton and zooplankton—which they study under a microscope. The team also use sensors to measure the sea temperature and nutrients in the water, to monitor conditions that allow the plankton to grow.

Phytoplankton are minute algae that use the sun's energy and nutrients dissolved in seawater to grow.

Zooplankton are all sorts of tiny animals. Some are the young larvae of fish, squid, and crabs. Others, like copepods, never grow any bigger.

The World's Most Famous Tortoise
LONESOME GEORGE

As the team sail past Pinta Island, Tomas remembers the island's most famous resident, Lonesome George.

In 1971, a scientist was studying snails on Pinta Island when he spotted a lone giant tortoise. This tortoise came to be known as Lonesome George.

It had been a long time since anyone had seen a tortoise on the island. People assumed the Pinta tortoises had already gone extinct. Centuries ago, whaling ships and fur seal traders moored at the Galápagos and helped themselves to live tortoises as a source of fresh meat for their long voyages.

Then, in the 1950s, fishers released three goats on Pinta Island, so there would be meat for them to hunt when they came back. But those three goats soon became 40,000! The goats munched their way through the island's plants and trees, which left very little for the remaining tortoises to eat.

Lonesome George was taken to a breeding center on Santa Cruz Island. There, a man called Fausto Llerena cared for George and came to think of him as a member of his family. Lonesome George became the emblem of the Galápagos and the most famous tortoise in the world.

Fausto and the other staff at the Galápagos National Park did their best to find a mate for George. They introduced him to female tortoises of closely related species. But he just wasn't interested!

In the end, there was nothing anyone could do to stop his species going extinct. After forty years on Santa Cruz, on June 24, 2012, it was Fausto who found George lying near his water pool inside his enclosure. He had died of natural causes.

Lonesome George was an endling: the last known individual of a species or subspecies.

EAVESDROPPING ON GIANTS

A group of enormous animals come to the Galápagos to make the most of the rich underwater feast. As the ship drifts through the open sea between the islands, Oscar puts down his hydrophones to listen for them.

Sperm whales communicate with clicking sounds. To a human ear they sound like a roll of tape unwinding, but much louder. Hundreds or thousands of sperm whales live together in groups known as clans. All the whales in a clan make similar patterns of clicks. It's like whale clans from different places talk with their own particular accent.

Each sperm whale has a specific call of repeated clicks (called a coda)*, like a name.*

Hello!

Sperm whale calls can be heard nearly a hundred miles away. They emit sounds from their enormous noses, which take up a third of their body—the biggest noses of any animal!

Whales with a Galápagos Accent

The patterns of sperm whale clicks that Oscar records are different to ones scientists recorded in the Galápagos 20 years ago. The whales haven't changed their accents but the clans have moved. Older clans left and two new clans have arrived—and nobody really knows why!

Let's go eat!

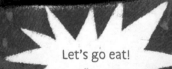

Understanding Whale Talk

But there's an even bigger puzzle Oscar wants to solve! What are the whales saying to each other? To help him decode their clicks, he records the whale sounds and films them at the same time. By listening and watching back as the whales dive and hunt and hang out together, Oscar is trying to work out what the patterns of clicks mean.

Follow me!

If sperm whales feel threatened by predators, like orca, they sometimes do emergency poos! The brown clouds in the water confuse the attackers and give the whales a chance to escape.

How are you?

Sperm whale
Cachalote

Size: 52–66 ft.
Lifespan: 70 years +
(v) Vulnerable

35

CYCLING CLIMATE CHANGES

A natural climate cycle affects the temperature and weather across the Pacific. Different phases of the cycle are called El Niño and La Niña.

During El Niño, currents in the Pacific Ocean change their course and the sea gets warmer, making conditions difficult for a lot of marine life. The sea can get so warm that corals growing in places like the Great Barrier Reef get stressed and die, a phenomenon known as coral bleaching.

The winds change.

El Niño brings more rain and storms to the Galápagos.

Forests of giant daisy trees get flattened and introduced blackberry brambles grow in their place.

Penguins, sea lions, cormorants, and marine iguanas have less to eat.

Fewer nutrients mean fewer fish.

Less seaweed.

The sea gets warmer.

Cold water upwelling gets weaker.

Animals in Peril

After El Niño events, animals around the Galápagos have been hit hard. In 1983, 77% of the penguins died. In 1998, 90% of marine iguanas on some islands died. There have been three "super" El Niño events in the last 40 years: 1982–83, 1997–98, and 2015–16. Scientists predict that climate change will make El Niño happen more often.

El Niño

La Niña has the opposite effect of El Niño.

Penguins, sea lions, cormorants, and marine iguanas have plenty to eat.

More seaweed.

More nutrients and fish.

Upwelling restarts.

The sea cools.

La Niña

LONG-DISTANCE WANDERERS

At the far southeast corner of the Galápagos, the *Sula* arrives at Española Island. This is the only place in the world where waved albatrosses raise their young. For much of the year, these enormous birds soar over the ocean, roaming huge distances hunting for fish. But now the mating season is in full swing and the *Sula* science team set about counting the thousands of newly hatched chicks.

Their name comes from the wave pattern on the adults' wings.

Females lay a single egg, which takes up to 2 months to hatch.

Waved albatross
Albatros de Galápagos

Wingspan: 8 ft.
Lifespan: 30 years
CE Critically Endangered

Stages of the Albatross Life Cycle:

1. When they're five and a half months old, chicks learn to fly, using the steep cliffs to launch themselves into the sky.

2. Once they have fledged, young albatrosses spend 6 years at sea before returning to Española to find a mate.

3. Waved albatrosses stay with one partner throughout their life.

– Española Island –

One of the oldest islands in the Galápagos—3.5 million years old
Area: 23 mi²
Highest point: 675 ft.
Human population: 0

RETURN OF THE GIANTS

From afar, it looks like there are boulders scattered across Española Island. Actually, this is the result of one of the world's most successful captive breeding programs, which brought Española tortoises back from the brink of extinction. Just like Lonesome George, the tortoises of Española got in big trouble because goats demolished their habitat and ate their favorite food—prickly pear cactus trees. But this story has a much happier ending!

The story starts in the 1960s when there were only 15 Española giant tortoises left. One was a male called Diego. He was taken along with the 14 other tortoises to a breeding center where they started producing babies—lots of babies.

Diego is father to more than 1,000 baby tortoises!

Española giant tortoise
Tortuga gigante de Española

Size: 5-6 ft.
Lifespan: 100 years +
CE Critically Endangered

When the young tortoises were big enough to fend for themselves, they were taken to Española and set free. There are now more than 2,300 tortoises roaming around the island, all the children and grandchildren of Diego and the other original tortoises.

Along with helping the tortoises to breed, conservationists have also been replanting endangered prickly pear cactus trees on Española and removing the goats that eat them. So now the tortoises should do okay by themselves.

As for Diego and his friends, they are still around too—giant tortoises can live for more than 100 years! In 2020, they were brought back to their home on Española.

Darwin in Galápagos
CHARLES DARWIN

This is San Cristobal, the island where Charles Darwin first set foot in the Galápagos. It's amazing to think he was here nearly 200 years ago, as part of his awesome scientific journey around the world. The Galápagos totally blew his mind. He saw plants and animals completely different to anything he'd seen anywhere else.

Darwin thought marine iguanas were ugly, but also very interesting. To find out more about their feeding habits he picked one up and chucked it in a tide pool hoping he could watch it eating. But the iguana just climbed out and walked back over to where Darwin stood.

So Darwin chased the iguana back to the sea . . .

And it clambered out again!

Darwin was very fond of the giant tortoises. He would sit on them as they slowly plodded around and he tried not to fall off. (Riding giant tortoises is definitely not allowed these days.) When he wasn't riding them, Darwin watched the giant tortoises and calculated they could walk 180 feet in ten minutes, which is nearly 4.5 miles a day (if they don't stop walking)!

But Darwin wasn't just someone who liked riding tortoises and flinging iguanas. He was a big thinker. All the time he traveled around the world he was thinking about how species look different and how they survive. Back in England, he thought about the Galápagos for a long time, and did lots more research, until he came up with an idea that totally changed the world . . .

Darwin arrived in the
Galápagos on September 16,
1835, and stayed for 5 weeks.

LABORATORY OF EVOLUTION

More than twenty years after Darwin left the Galápagos, he finished writing one of the most famous science books of all time. *On the Origin of Species* explains Darwin's theory of how species evolve and how the world is filled with so many different animals and plants. The wildlife he saw in the Galápagos was a big inspiration for these ideas.

Darwin realized that animals and plants living in the Galápagos must have originally come from South America. Some animals flew, some swam, some drifted on logs. Plants arrived as seeds stuck to birds' feet or blown by the wind. Gradually the new arrivals adapted to the local conditions.

Living in the hot climate near the equator, Galápagos penguins evolved to be smaller and have fewer feathers than their ancestors. The penguins also learned to shade their black feet with their flippers to keep cool.

In the Galápagos, individual penguins didn't shrink and individual cormorants didn't get shorter wings. Instead, over generations, the average size of penguins' bodies and cormorants' wings got smaller.

When cormorants arrived in the Galápagos there were no land predators trying to catch them. The birds no longer needed to fly. Over time their wings evolved to be shorter and shorter until they became flightless. They save energy by swimming instead.

Darwin's book explained how new species evolve by gradual changes over millions of years in a process called *natural selection*. Organisms best suited to local conditions are the ones that survive and pass on their useful characters to their offspring. Over time, separate species evolve that look and behave differently from each other.

Another Big Thinker

Alfred Russell Wallace was another great scientist who came up with a very similar theory of evolution at the same time as Darwin. He got his ideas studying wildlife on the islands of Indonesia.

BEAKS OF FINCHES

An important group of little birds helped inspire Darwin's theory of evolution. Scientists still go to the Galápagos to study them and learn more about how species change and evolve. Across the Galápagos there are fourteen species of finches that all have different beaks.

Some have big, blunt beaks, which are good for crushing tough seeds.

Some have smaller beaks, which are good for eating small seeds and sipping nectar from flowers.

Some have beaks that are good for picking up twigs and digging insects out of tree bark.

Evolution in Action

Every year, for forty years, Rosemary and Peter Grant went to study finches on the tiny island of Daphne Major. They took their two daughters with them, Thalia and Nicola, from when they were 6 and 8 years old. The girls made friends with a sea lion cub, played violin for the blue-footed boobies, and helped with the scientific studies. Over the years, the Grants saw the finches' beaks changing. The birds were beginning to evolve into new species.

After a bad drought in 1977 only big seeds were available. Only finches with big beaks were able to eat these seeds. The next generations inherited bigger beaks from those surviving birds. Gradually, the finches' beaks got bigger.

In 1982, El Niño struck. It poured with rain, vines grew all over Daphne Major, and there were loads of fruit and seeds. This time, the surviving finches were the ones with smaller beaks that are better for eating smaller, softer seeds. After El Niño, the finches' beaks got smaller.

The Grants saw evolution happening right before their eyes, much faster than anyone expected—not over millions of years but within just a few years and a few generations of birds. Charles Darwin would have been totally amazed!

DIVING ON THE DEVIL'S CROWN

The *Sula* sails to the north side of Floreana Island and drops anchor near the Devil's Crown. The scuba-diving scientists carry out a survey around this old volcanic crater, which looks like a crown sticking up from the waves. Underwater is a bustling coral ecosystem. Their aim is to study how well the corals are growing.

Ember parrotfish

Starfish and sea urchins

Blue chin parrotfish

King angelfish

Razor surgeonfish

Blacknosed butterflyfish

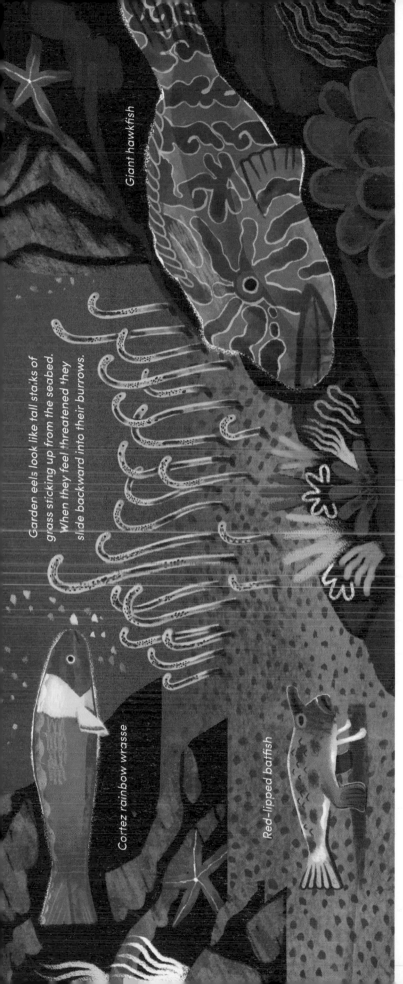

Garden eels look like tall stalks of grass sticking up from the seabed. When they feel threatened they slide backward into their burrows.

Giant hawkfish

Cortez rainbow wrasse

Red-lipped batfish

By taking snapshots of the same areas of reef that have been photographed in previous years, the *Sula* scientists track how corals are changing over time.

The Galápagos is a tough place for corals to grow. Normally they prefer stable, warm conditions but here the temperature keeps changing, especially when El Niño comes along.

In 1982–83, El Niño wiped out 90% of corals in Galápagos. Corals got hot and stressed and lost the colorful algae living inside them, making them bleach white and die.

Coral before 1982–83

Coral after 1982–83

Seeing into the Future

Corals don't like acid. It makes it tough to grow their chalky skeletons. At Devil's Crown the sea is naturally acidic because carbon dioxide rises up from below. But still corals survive here. Studying these corals, scientists see what the future might hold for corals in the rest of the ocean when it gets more acidic (by absorbing more carbon dioxide released by burning fossil fuels).

INTO THE DAISY FOREST

On Floreana, the *Sula* team explore the forest of giant daisy trees and search for endangered species. Fifty-four species on the island are at risk of going extinct. Some have already disappeared, and only survive in small numbers on other islands in the Galápagos.

Floreana mockingbird
Cucuve de Floreana

Size: 10 in.
Lifespan: Unknown
(EN) Endangered
(EX) Extinct on Floreana

Charles Darwin found four species of mockingbirds in the Galápagos, which helped him work out his theory of evolution. The mockingbirds disappeared from Floreana not long after Darwin visited. Mockingbirds copy the sounds of other animals—but the mockingbirds in the Galápagos don't mock! It's one of the changes that happened after their ancestors moved to the islands.

Darwin's flycatcher
Pájaro brujo

Size: 5 in.
Lifespan: 5 years
(V) Vulnerable
(EX) Extinct on Floreana

Darwin collected flycatchers during his visit to the Galápagos. Males are black and red. The grey and yellow females are harder to spot. This species is extinct on Floreana but still live on a few other Galápagos islands.

Giant daisy trees are big shrubs that are in the same family as daisies. Daisy forests grow in the mountains where mist called *garua* hangs in the air. The forests are threatened by habitat loss as trees are cut down to make way for farms.

Giant daisy trees
Árbol de la margarita

Size: 66 ft.
Lifespan: 25 years
V Vulnerable

Land snails
Galapagos caracol de terra

Size: Up to 1 in.
Lifespan: Unknown
CE 3 species Critically Endangered;
EN 6 Endangered;
V 4 Vulnerable

Floreana has 20 endemic species and 8 subspecies of land snails. They all breathe air. Threats include rats and mice that eat these snails and their eggs.

Galápagos petrel
Petrel de Galápagos

Wingspan: 36 in.
Lifespan: Unknown
CE Critically Endangered

Galápagos petrels build nests underground. They used to nest across the Galápagos. Now 60% are on Floreana. Threats include dogs, pigs, and cats that catch them. El Niño events can affect their food supply. They're also threatened by marine plastic pollution.

LAVA SHORES

On Pinzón Island, the *Sula* scientists encounter more animals that live only in the Galápagos. Down by the waterline, lava herons hunt for crabs, catching two or three every minute. Pinzón lava lizards, a species endemic just to this island, skitter across the rocks. They defend their territories by doing push-ups, which helps them look big and strong and scares off other lizards. The team observe the animals on Pinzón's shore and document their behavior.

Lava heron
Garza de lava

Size: 14–25 in.
Lifespan: Unknown
LC Least Concern

Pinzón lava lizards
Lagartija de lava

Size: 8–12 in.
Lifespan: 10 years
NT Near Threatened

Sally lightfoot crabs
Zapaya

Size: 2-3 in.
Lifespan: Unknown
LC Least Concern

53

SALTY, SWIMMING LIZARDS

On Santiago Island, the *Sula* team survey the population of marine iguanas as they bask in the sun on the rocky shore. Marine iguanas are the only lizards in the world that live and feed in the sea, and they're endemic to the Galápagos. Scientists used to think there were seven very similar subspecies living on different islands, but new studies of their DNA show there are actually eleven.

Marine iguanas are good swimmers and sometimes swim all the way between islands. The new arrivals breed successfully with the local population and mix things up. That seems to be what stops new species from forming on each island.

Marine iguanas have glands in their noses that get rid of the excess salt they eat while feeding. They have very salty sneezes!

Their long, powerful claws help them climb out of the sea and grip onto the lava rocks.

Marine iguanas are herbivores. They hold their breath and dive underwater to munch on red and green seaweed. Their flattened tails help them swim.

Marine iguanas listen and run for cover when they hear a mockingbird's alarm call that signals a hunting hawk is nearby. Hawks catch birds and iguanas.

During the mating season, male iguanas change from black to bright colors. Each subspecies has a different set of mating colors.

Young marine iguanas eat the droppings of older iguanas—and for a good reason! Adult marine iguanas have bacteria in their stomachs that help them digest seaweed. By eating the droppings, the young iguanas get a dose of helpful bacteria.

Marine iguana
Iguana marina

Size: 2-5 ft.
Lifespan: 5-12 years
Ⓥ Vulnerable

55

RED BEACH AND FLAMINGOS

On Rábida Island, the *Sula* crew hike to an inland lagoon to study a flock of pink flamingos. The scientists want to find out how El Niño is affecting the birds and their favorite food—tiny crustaceans called brine shrimp. The team measures the concentration of salt in the lagoon, study the brine shrimp, and count the flamingos.

During an El Niño event it can rain so much the lakes and pools in the Galápagos become less salty from all the freshwater pouring down. This is bad news for brine shrimp, which like it to be salty. But, unlike penguins and flightless cormorants, flamingos don't have to stay put when El Niño ruins their food. They can fly off and find somewhere better to feed.

These lanky-legged flamingos feed with their heads upside down, swinging their beaks from side to side to filter brine shrimp from the water. They have strainers inside their mouths, a bit like humpbacks and other baleen whales.

Flamingo
Flamenco del Caribe

Size: 4–4.5 ft.
Lifespan: 60 years
LC Least Concern

Flamingos are found on 42 lakes across the Galápagos on Rábida, Santiago, Isabela, Floreana, and Santa Cruz.

57

THE BLUER THE BETTER

At North Seymour Island, the *Sula* team arrive to monitor some of the most colorful seabirds in the Galápagos. Around the islands, blue-footed boobies are having trouble breeding. It seems they haven't been very good at laying eggs and rearing their young. The population has been getting smaller and smaller. To understand what's happening to the birds, Davide and the other scientists count the boobies and their chicks. These numbers will be added to the annual surveys that monitor the booby population over time.

Blue-footed boobies have a funny courtship ritual that begins when a male presents a female with a small stone or stick.

Then he points his beak, tail, and wing tips toward the sky and he whistles.

Then he stomps around the female, showing off his beautiful blue feet. Females pick males with the brightest, bluest feet. They are the ones in the best condition and make the best mates.

Fifty years ago, there were around 20,000 blue-footed boobies in the Galápagos. There are now only around 6,400. It's possible the boobies aren't finding enough sardines to feed to their young.

Red-footed booby

Three species of booby live in the Galápagos: blue-footed, red-footed, and nazca boobies. They are easy to tell apart from their colors.

Nazca booby

The blue color in their feet comes from pigments called carotenoids obtained from their food. Their name comes from the Spanish word bobo, which means silly.

Blue-footed booby
Piquero patas azules

Wingspan: 5 ft.
Lifespan: 17 years
LC Least Concern

– **North Seymour Island** –
Area: 0.7 mi²
Highest point: 92 ft.
Human population: 0

BLACK TURTLE COVE

A mangrove forest transforms the shores of Black Turtle Cove, or *Caleta Tortuga Negra*, on Santa Cruz Island, from sharp, rocky lava into a lush green ecosystem bursting with life. The *Sula* team divide up the tasks of studying above and below the waterline, to find out just how important these mangroves are.

Exploring the Underwater Forest

The team catalog the rich mix of animals that live around the mangroves. Lots of young fish hang out around the prop roots, hiding from predators until they grow big enough to venture into open water. Young sharks and turtles seek shelter and food in the mangroves too.

Mangroves cover a third of the coastlines around the Galápagos.

> **– Santa Cruz Island –**
> *Second biggest island in the Galápagos*
> *Size: 380 mi²*
> *Highest point: 2,835 ft.*
> *Human population: Approx. 12,000*

Measuring Muddy Carbon Stores

Cata, Tomas, and Davide count mangrove trees, collect fallen leaves and scoop up mud. Back in *Sula's* lab, they will work out the amount of carbon stored in the forest. In many other countries, people cut down mangroves, which releases the stored carbon as carbon dioxide gas. This adds to the problems of human-made climate change by trapping more of the sun's energy and heating the planet.

Estefania sends up a drone to photograph the mangrove forest from the air. The photos will help the team work out the size of the forest and calculate the total amount of carbon it stores in the mud, trunks, and leaves. The Galápagos is one of the few places in the world where mangrove forests are naturally growing larger. The more mangroves, the more carbon they lock up and keep out of the atmosphere.

Four species of mangrove trees grow in the Galápagos: White, black, red, and button mangrove.

UNDERWATER VOLCANO

At Roca Redonda, far off the north coast of Isabela Island, Cata the geologist, leads a very unusual scuba dive. All around them are bubbles of gas. It's like diving in a glass of champagne.

Roca Redonda is a steep, volcanic island that sticks up 200 feet above the water. It's all that's left of a 53,000-year-old volcano!

This is a rare underwater shield volcano that is still active. The gas bubbles are coming from openings in the volcano called *fumaroles*.

WATCHING HUGE, SPOTTY FISH

The *Sula* arrives at the most northerly part of the Galápagos—at Darwin and Wolf Islands. This is the best place in the Galápagos to see the world's biggest fish. Many of them are females with bulging bellies. This could be where whale sharks come to give birth, but nobody has found any evidence for that yet. The *Sula* team carefully get in the water to survey the magnificent whale sharks and keep an eye out for any small ones.

Spotting Sharks

Like Galápagos penguins, whale sharks have unique patterns. Leo photographs the whale sharks around Darwin's Arch. Later, she'll use her computer to automatically identify the patterns of spots and work out if these whale sharks have been seen here by scientists before. Using harmless laser beams, 10 inches apart, she accurately measures how long the sharks are.

Whale shark
Tiburón ballena

Size: Up to 66 ft.
Lifespan: 100 years +
EN Endangered

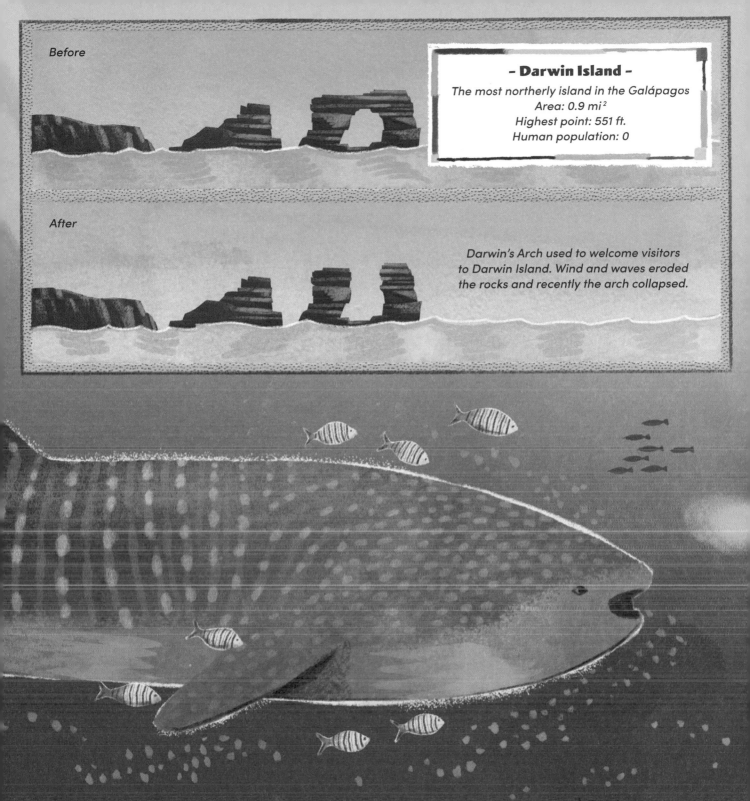

Before

After

Darwin's Arch used to welcome visitors to Darwin Island. Wind and waves eroded the rocks and recently the arch collapsed.

Whale sharks of the Galápagos go on long journeys for hundreds of miles across the Pacific. Hammerhead sharks, silky sharks, manta rays, sea turtles, and tuna swim along an underwater superhighway all the way from Darwin Island to Cocos Island. In 2021, at the climate summit in Glasgow, Scotland, the president of Ecuador announced plans to expand the Galápagos Marine Reserve including protecting the "Galápagos-Cocos Swimway," as it's known, to help conserve all these migrating animals.

DEEP-SEA MOUNTAINS

In the Galápagos there are hundreds of underwater volcanoes called seamounts. They can be 9,800 feet tall. The *Sula* team search for seamounts and study the mysterious ecosystems growing on them.

Seeing with Sound

A sonar device on the *Sula* sends out sound pulses that bounce off the seabed. The machine detects echoes coming back and a computer transforms them into a 3D map. This helps the team locate seamounts and decide where to dive.

Diving into the Deep

Estefania, Ren, and Cata climb inside the deep-diving submersible, *Kiwa*, and get ready for their first dive. A crane lifts the sub off the *Sula* and lowers it into the sea. Inside, Estefania takes the controls and steers the sub into the deep.

Growing all over the seamount are weird-shaped creatures that look like plants. In fact they're animals, including many species that nobody has ever seen before. These are corals and sponges and they can live for a very long time. There are bamboo corals that were already growing here around the time Charles Darwin visited the Galápagos almost 200 years ago.

Black corals are some of the world's oldest-known animals. They grow on seamounts and can live for more than 4,000 years!

Just like forests on land, seamount forests are home to all sorts of other animals. There are octopuses and fish, starfish, sea urchins, and squat lobsters.

Collecting Rocks, New Species, and Medicines

The scientists use *Kiwa*'s robotic arms to take small samples of rocks to learn how the volcanic seamount formed. They also snip small pieces of corals and sponges to bring back and study. This will help Ren identify new species. The corals and sponges might also contain chemicals that could be useful for making new medicines.

EXPLORING EXTREME LIFE

Inside the submersible *Kiwa*, Ren, Estefania, and Cata go on another dive, this time even deeper, several hundred feet down, to study an ecosystem that works in a totally different way to anything else on Earth.

Hydrothermal vents form wherever seawater seeps through cracks in the deep seabed and gets heated by hot magma chambers below. The hot water gushes back up and pours out of chimneys, which are sometimes called black smokers. Vents can reach hundreds of degrees but the super high pressure so far underwater stops the seawater from boiling.

Seeking Species

More than 700 species have been found on hydrothermal vents in deep seas all around the world. Eight out of ten of them are endemic, they only live on vents. Often when studying vents, scientists find new species. Ren searches around these black smokers for animals that nobody has seen before.

Pompeii worms live in tubes stuck right on the chimneys. They are some of the world's most heatproof animals!

Giant tube worms grow taller than a fully grown human. They keep microbes in a special pouch inside their bodies.

Egg Warmer

A short way from the scorching vent, the scientists inside *Kiwa* see something they weren't expecting: a huge pile of egg cases. Giant deep-water skates (flattened cousins of sharks) have laid their eggs near the vent, where the seawater is not too hot and not too cold, but just the right temperature to incubate them until they hatch.

Yeti crabs grow chemical-loving microbes on their furry arms. The crabs crawl near the hydrothermal vents to make sure the microbes get enough chemicals to grow. When the crabs get hungry, they eat the microbes growing in their fur!

How Chemosynthesis Works

Instead of using sunlight to grow, microbes use toxic chemicals pouring out of the vent chimneys.

Microbes inside tube worms harness energy from these chemicals.

Discovering Life in the Dark

Scientists first saw hydrothermal vents in 1977, diving near the Galápagos in a submersible called *Alvin*. This led to a groundbreaking discovery. Until then, scientists thought all living creatures need the sun for survival. Plants and algae carry out photosynthesis, using sunlight to grow and make food. Then animals eat the plants, or other plant-eating animals. But on hydrothermal vents, food comes from microbes that don't use photosynthesis, but a process called chemosynthesis. The whole ecosystem can survive in the total darkness and doesn't need any sunlight at all.

SHARK POINT

Rising back up toward the surface, the scientists inside *Kiwa* find themselves surrounded by all sorts of shark, including some rare ones. Sixgill and sevengill sharks are hardly ever seen in the Galápagos.

Sixgill sharks
Boca dolça

Size: 15 ft.
Lifespan: Unknown
(NT) Near Threatened

The sea surrounding Darwin and Wolf Islands in the Galápagos is home to the largest concentration of sharks on earth. All these predators are able to live together because there's plenty to eat from all the prey that feast in these plankton-rich waters. The sharks are also protected from fishing inside the marine reserve.

Tool Heads

Kiwa rises up through a huge shoal of scalloped hammerhead sharks. These sharks live in coastal areas around the world but the Galápagos is the only place where hundreds of them regularly gather in huge schools. Why they form these schools remains a mystery!

Their weird head or cephalofoil helps the hammerhead sharks to see. The view through each eye overlaps in the middle giving them excellent stereoscopic vision, which means they're good at working out how far away things are. Hammerheads can expertly strike from just the right distance to snap up prey. They also have sensitive pores all over their heads, called ampullae of Lorenzini, which detect weak electric fields generated by an animal's muscles.

Scalloped hammerheads
Tiburón martillo

Size: 14 ft.
Lifespan: 35 years
CE Critically Endangered

Sevengill sharks
Tiburón de siete gallas

Size: 10 ft.
Lifespan: 49 years +
V Vulnerable

– Wolf Island –
Area: 1.1 mi²
Highest point: 830 ft.
Human population: 0

JOURNEY'S END

Now that the expedition has come to an end the science team has an important job to do. They'll be helping to spread the word about the amazing wildlife around the islands and the environmental challenges they face. And that's how you can help too!

The pink iguana numbers haven't increased. They need help before the volcano erupts again.
The young penguins are doing well.
You'll never guess how many sunfish we saw!
There are sixgill *and* sevengill sharks down there!
These coral samples were growing half a mile underwater!
Darwin's Arch has fallen down! Can you believe it?

WHAT DOES THE FUTURE HOLD FOR THE GALÁPAGOS?

The Galápagos is a living treasure trove and a remote hideaway for so much life. But there are still problems. Some islands are missing species that were lost when habitats were destroyed or they were hunted by introduced predators, such as rats and cats. The good news is that island wildlife can quickly recover when people lend a helping hand. Now, conservationists are working hard to rewild more of the Galápagos and reintroduce all sorts of wonderful species that were thought to be lost forever.

Young Floreana mockingbirds will be moved from Gardner and Champion Islets to Floreana Island to establish new territories.

In 2019, conservationists found a single Fernandina giant tortoise, a species thought to have gone extinct. Now, the search is on for more Fernandina tortoises for her to breed with.

Conservationists are rearing baby tortoises that are a close match to the extinct Floreana giant tortoises. Their ancestors come from Isabela Island where, centuries ago, tortoises washed up after a ship sank that was carrying live tortoises from Floreana. The shipwreck survivors bred with Isabela's tortoises, creating hybrids.

Other animals that could be reintroduced to their former ranges around the Galápagos:

Five species of finch including mangrove finches

Darwin's flycatchers

Lava gulls

Galápagos racers

Galápagos barn owls

Galápagos hawks

Galápagos rail

GLOSSARY

A

Archipelago: A collection of islands

B

Bacteria: Tiny organisms (or living things) that can be found in all natural environments

Biodiversity: The variety of plant and animal life in the world, or in a particular habitat

C

Cartilage: Firm, flexible tissue that makes up the skeletons of some fish, like sharks

Crater: A hole, produced by a meteorite, volcanic activity, or an explosion

Currents: A body of fluid, like water or air, moving in a specific direction

E

Ecosystem: All the living things, including plants and animals, that are living in a certain area

Equator: The imaginary line around the earth that separates the northern and southern halves, or hemispheres, of the earth

Erode: To wear away

Evolution: The theory that all kinds of living things that exist today developed from past organisms

Evolve: To develop or change by steps

F

Fossil fuels: Natural substances like coal or gas, which humans burn for fuel

H

Hydrothermal: Relating to extremely hot water

I

Incubate: To keep (eggs) warm until it's time to hatch

M

Mangrove: Trees or bushes that grow in thick clusters along seashores and riverbanks

Microbe: A living thing, including bacteria, that cannot be seen with the naked eye

Migration: When animals move on a regular cycle

Migratory: To move from one region to another

P

Parasite: An organism, or living thing, that lives on or inside another organism

Photosynthesis: The process in which green plants and algae use sunlight to make their own food

Pigments: A substance that gives color to other materials

S

Shoal: A place where a sea, lake, or river is shallow, also a group of fish swimming together

Species: A group that contains all of a certain type of animal, plant, or other organism with the same characteristics

Specimen: A sample of something

Subspecies: A group within a species that has become genetically and usually physically different from the rest of the group

T

Territory: The area an animal consistently defends against other animals

U

Upwelling: A process in which currents bring deep, cold water to the surface of the ocean

INDEX

Written by Helen Scales

Helen Scales is a writer, marine biologist, broadcaster and scuba diver whose work focuses on oceans and their inhabitants. She has a masters degree in Tropical Coastal Management from Newcastle University, and a PhD from Cambridge University, UK.

Illustrated by Rômolo D'Hipólito

Rômolo D'Hipólito is a Brazilian artist and illustrator. In 2019, he received the Special Mention Award at Golden Pinwheel Young Illustrators Competition, and in 2018, he was selected for the Ibero-America official catalog.

Next in the series . . .

Join a team of scientists on a trip across Antarctica. Learn all about the incredible creatures both above and below the ice from elephant seals to emperor penguins and orcas to ice fish and discover how scientists work in this extreme and changing environment, studying climate change, ice cores, conservation, and more.